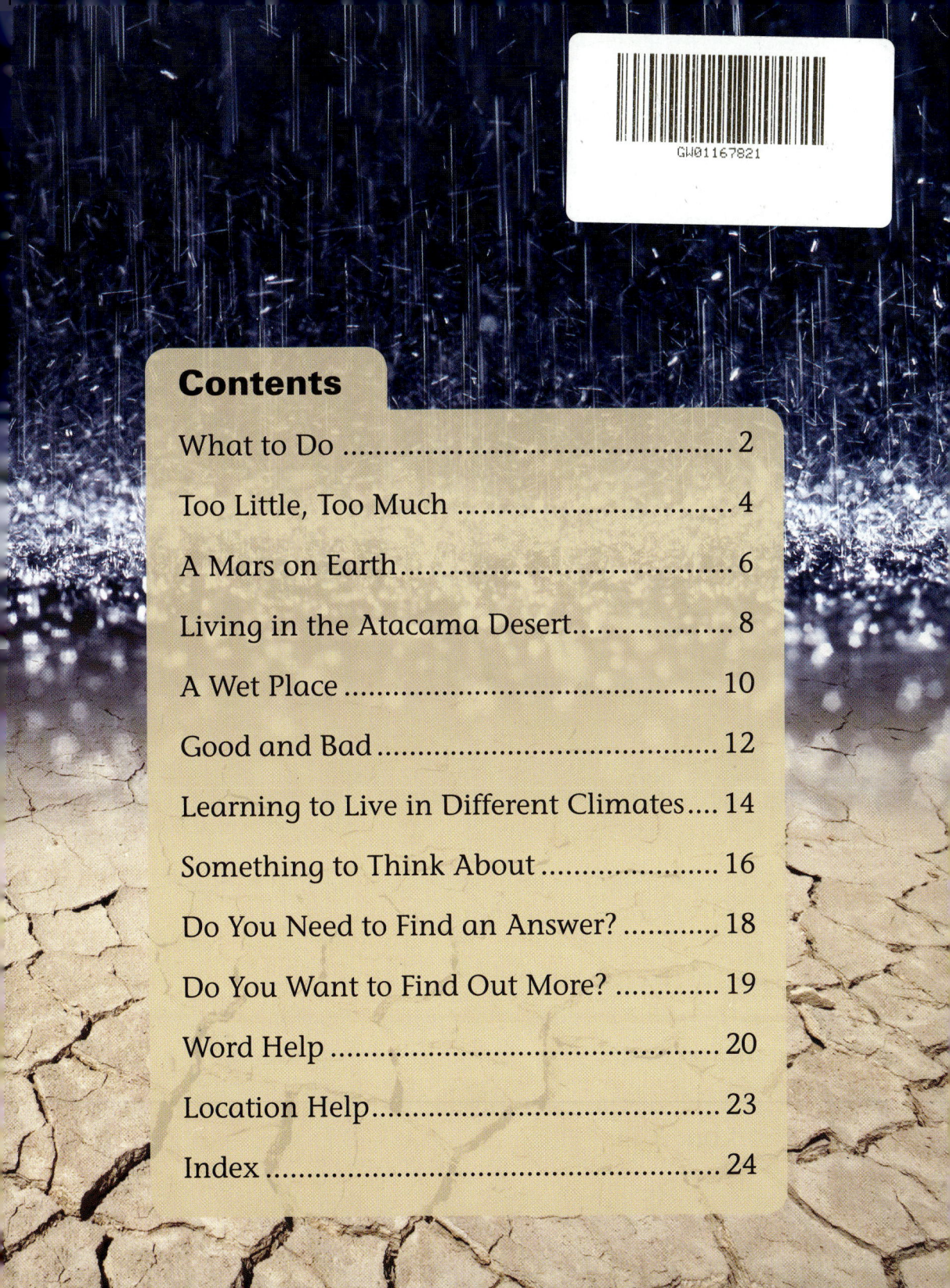

Contents

What to Do 2

Too Little, Too Much 4

A Mars on Earth 6

Living in the Atacama Desert 8

A Wet Place 10

Good and Bad 12

Learning to Live in Different Climates 14

Something to Think About 16

Do You Need to Find an Answer? 18

Do You Want to Find Out More? 19

Word Help 20

Location Help 23

Index 24

What to Do

Choose a face

Remember the colour you have chosen.

When you see your face on the page, you are the LEADER.

The LEADER reads the text in the speech bubbles.

There are extra words and questions to help you on the teacher's whiteboard. The LEADER reads these aloud.

When you see this stop sign, the LEADER reads it aloud.

STOP
My predictions were right/wrong because . . .

You might need:

- to look at the WORD HELP on pages 20–22;
- to look at the LOCATION HELP on page 23;
- an atlas.

If you are the **LEADER**, follow these steps:

1 PREDICT

Think about what is on the page.

- Say to your group:

"I am looking at this page and I think it is going to be about…"

- Tell your group:

"Read the page to yourselves."

2 CLARIFY

Talk about words and their meaning.

- Say to your group:

"Are there any words you don't know?"

"Is there anything else on the page you didn't understand?"

- Talk about the words and their meanings with your group.
- Read the whiteboard.

- Ask your group to find the LET'S CHECK word in the WORD HELP on pages 20–22. Ask them to read the meaning of the word aloud.

3 ASK QUESTIONS

Talk about how to find out more.

- Say to your group:

"Who has a question about what we have read?"

- Question starters are: how…, why…, when…, where…, what…, who…
- Read the question on the whiteboard and talk about it with your group.

4 SUMMARISE

Think about who and what the story was mainly about.

When you get to pages 16–17, you can talk to a partner or write and draw on your own.

 or

Too Little, Too Much

Some places in the world are dry, and it hardly rains at all. In other places, it can rain for months without stopping. Too little rain, or too much rain, can cause problems for living things.

The **environment** in a dry place looks different from one that gets lots of rain.

One of the driest places on Earth is the Atacama Desert. Some places in this desert haven't had any rain for hundreds of years.

I am looking at this page and I think it is going to be about… because…

Are there any words you don't know?

Let's check: environment

Who has a question about what we have read?

How do you think the environment in wet places is different from in dry places?

Many parts of the Atacama Desert are so dry that there are huge cracks in the land.

A Mars on Earth

In the Atacama Desert there is no **moisture** in the air, so there are very few clouds. This makes Atacama a good place to look at the stars.

Some people think that parts of this desert don't look like Earth at all. Scientists have set up a space station here. They think that the land is a lot like the land on Mars. In the parts of the desert that are very dry, there is no life at all.

I am looking at this page and I think it is going to be about… because…

Are there any words you don't know?

Let's check: moisture

Who has a question about what we have read?

Why do you think this place might be like Mars?

Living in the Atacama Desert

Animals, plants, and even people, do live in the Atacama Desert. They have found ways to **survive**.

There is little water, but fog **drifts** in from the ocean. People use nets to catch the fog. The fog clings to the net, then the water drips down the net, into **troughs**.

In a dry place like Atacama, nothing **rots**. People have found **mummies** buried in the sand and salt. Some of the mummies are thousands of years old.

I am looking at this page and I think it is going to be about… because…

Are there any words you don't know?

Let's check: mummies

Who has a question about what we have read?

Why do you think getting water with a fog net might be difficult?

A Wet Place

One of the wettest places on Earth is in the East Khasi Hills in India. Here it rains for many months of the year. People go for a long time without seeing the sun. Then, after all the rain, there is a **drought**.

During the **monsoon season** it is very hard for people to go outside. The rain can come down sideways because of the winds. Some say it comes down in such thick sheets, you can't even see the drops.

I am looking at this page and I think it is going to be about… because…

Are there any words you don't know?

Let's check: monsoon

Who has a question about what we have read?

What do you think might be hard about living in such a wet place?

Keeping dry in the monsoon rain can be very difficult.

This page was mainly about fact fact

STOP
My predictions were right/wrong because . . .

Good and Bad

I am looking at this page and I think it is going to be about… because…

So much rain falling for so long causes problems for the people who live in the East Khasi Hills.

There can be floods. Roads can turn into rivers. It is hard to grow anything, because the rain washes seeds and crops away. Also, it washes away the good **topsoil**. The rain brings insects and **diseases**. It makes many things rot.

The rain has, however, **carved** out beautiful waterfalls and caves. People come from all over the world to **explore** them.

Are there any words you don't know?

Let's check: topsoil

Who has a question about what we have read?

How do you think the rain has carved out waterfalls and caves?

Learning to Live in Different Climates

I am looking at this page and I think it is going to be about… because…

The **climate** is very important to every living thing. Some climates can **provide** too much of one thing, but not enough of something else. Living things have to learn how to survive in the climate they live in.

In hot deserts, some animals live underground. An underground house might work well for people who live in hot places. But, in a place where it rains for months, an underground house might not be such a good idea at all.

Are there any words you don't know?

Who has a question about what we have read?

Let's check: climate

Why might it be hard to live in an underground house?

14

Something to Think About

 or

Living in a wet place

+

−

Think about the good things and the bad things about living in wet and dry places. Talk about your ideas with a partner, or write them down.

Living in a dry place

Do You Need to Find an Answer?

You could go to . . .

Do You Want to Find Out More?

You could look in books or on the internet using these key words to help you:

Atacama Desert

cave homes

East Khasi Hills

monsoon season

Word Help

Dictionary

carved	cut out
climate	the type of weather that a place usually has
diseases	illnesses, sicknesses
drifts	moves gently along by water or air
drought	a long time of very dry weather without rain
environment	everything around that surrounds a living thing
explore	to look carefully around a place to learn about it
moisture	dampness
monsoon	a very heavy wind and rainfall

mummies	the bodies of people or animals from long ago that have not rotted
provide	to give something that is needed
rots	goes bad
season	a part of the year when there is a particular type of weather
survive	to stay alive
topsoil	the soil on the top or the ground that is good for growing plants
troughs	long, narrow, open containers

Word Help

Thesaurus

buried	hidden
clings	grips, sticks
drips	dribbles, trickles
hardly	barely, scarcely
living	existing
thick	broad, wide, heavy

Location Help

The Driest Place, the Wettest Place

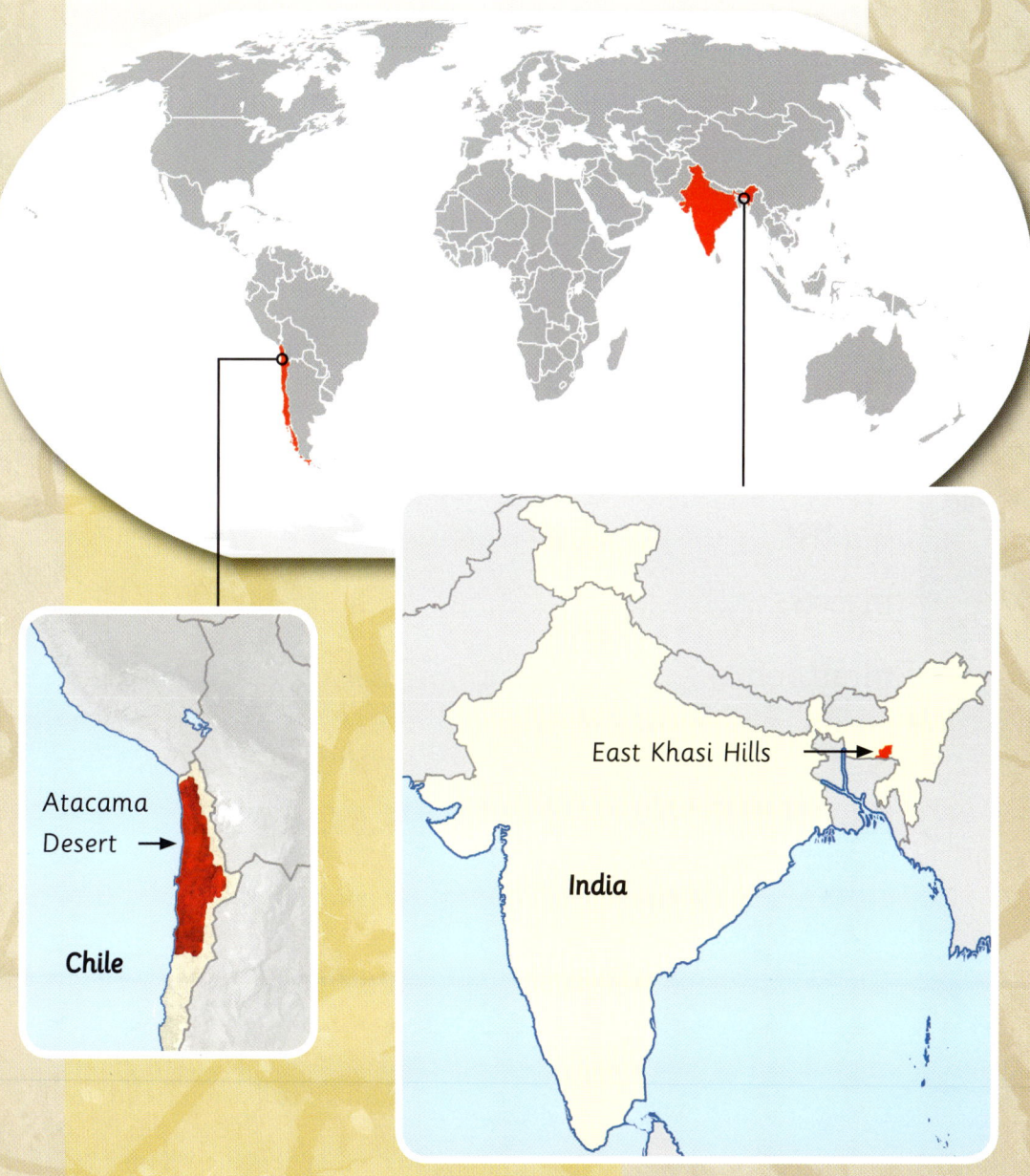

Index

Atacama Desert 4–5, 6–7, 8–9

caves.. 12, 14–15

climate 14

diseases.. 12

drought.. 10

East Khasi Hills 10–11, 12–13

floods... 12

fog nets.. 8–9

insects.. 12

monsoon 10–11

mummies 8–9

rain... 4, 10–11, 12, 14

stars 6

waterfalls 12–13